Loud or Soft? High or Low?
A Look at Sound

Jennifer Boothroyd

Lerner Publications
Minneapolis

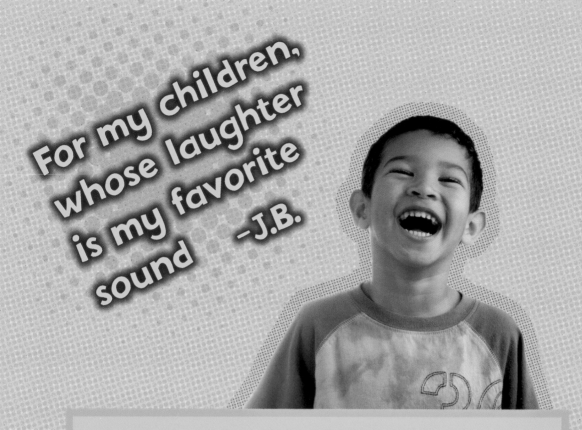

For my children,
whose laughter
is my favorite
sound —J.B.

Lerner Publications Company
A division of Lerner Publishing Group, Inc.
241 First Avenue North
Minneapolis, MN 55401 USA

For reading levels and more information, look up this title at www.lernerbooks.com.

Library of Congress Cataloging-in-Publication Data

Boothroyd, Jennifer, 1972-
        Loud or soft? High or low? : a look at sound / by Jennifer Boothroyd.
            p.   cm. — (Lightning bolt books ™— Exploring physical science)
        Includes index.
         ISBN 978-0-7613-6091-9 (lib. bdg. : alk. paper)
         ISBN 978-0-7613-7224-0 (EB pdf)
         1. Sound—Juvenile literature. 2. Sound-waves—Juvenile literature. I. Title.
        QC225.5.B648 2011
        534—dc22   2010017065

Manufactured in the United States of America
3 - 38540 - 11447 - 4/1/2016

Contents

What Is Sound?

Sounds are all around us. A dog barks. A bell rings. A motor hums. All this sound is a form of energy.

We hear sound when something vibrates, or moves back and forth. The vibrations travel in waves. Our ears catch the waves and hear the sound.

How Sound Travels

Sound waves travel in all directions.

You can hear fireworks boom and crackle from anywhere nearby.

Sound reflects, or bounces, off objects. An echo is a reflected sound.

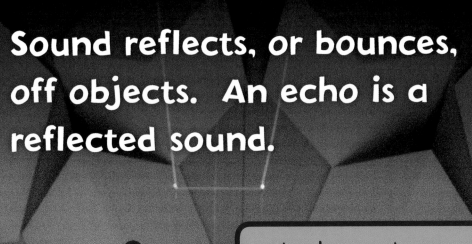

The large shapes on this wall reflect the sounds that instruments make. The shapes help fill the room with music.

Sound waves can travel through solid objects. You can hear a knock through a wooden door.

Sound waves can also travel through gases. The air is made of many gases. A police siren's wail travels in the air for several blocks.

Dolphins talk underwater through squeaks, clicks, and other noises.

Sound can travel through liquids too. Many animals make noises to communicate with one another underwater.

Pitch

Pitch describes how low or high a sound is. The sound of two glasses clinking has a high pitch. The roar of a lion has a low pitch.

The faster something vibrates, the higher the pitch. The slower it vibrates, the lower the pitch.

Blow air into a whistle slowly. Then blow faster. The whistle should have a higher pitch the second time because it is vibrating faster.

An object's length can also change its pitch. The shorter keys on a xylophone make higher sounds than the longer keys.

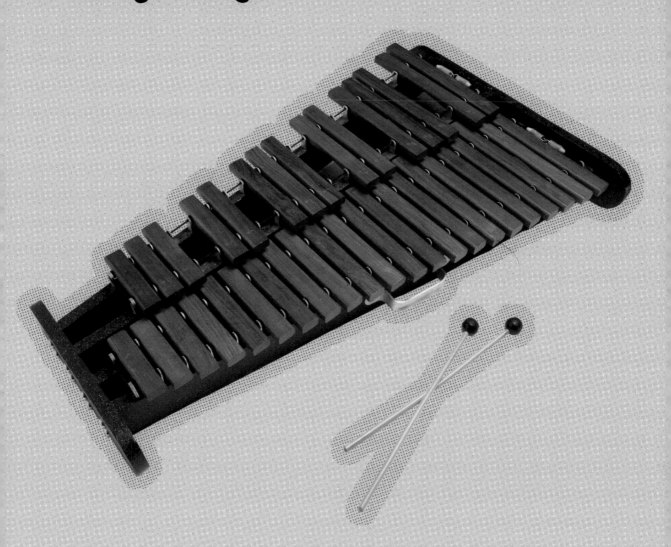

A tuba makes a very low sound. The air travels a long way through the instrument. Air travels a short way through a flute. This instrument makes a higher sound.

This boy's tuba makes a much lower sound than his bandmate's flute.

Guitar and violin players push down on the strings of the instruments to change notes. When they hold down a string, the part of the string that vibrates is shorter. The string vibrates faster. The pitch is higher.

Volume

Quiet or *loud* describes a sound's volume.

You need to use a quiet voice in the library.

You can use a loud voice
when you play outside.

You can change the volume of a TV to make it quieter or louder. But what can make a sound seem louder without a volume button or dial?

A megaphone can! That's because a sound is louder when sound waves are focused. Sound waves become less powerful as they spread out in the air. A megaphone helps focus sound waves.

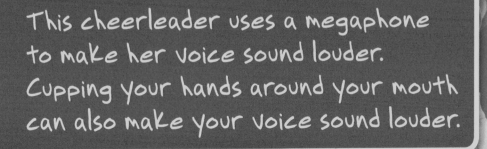

This cheerleader uses a megaphone to make her voice sound louder. Cupping your hands around your mouth can also make your voice sound louder.

You can hear a quiet sound nearby. But it's harder to hear a quiet sound from far away. The sound waves spread out too much.

How Sounds Are Made

To make a sound, an object must vibrate. There are many ways to make vibrations.

These cymbals make a sound when they are hit.

The force from a push can make an object vibrate.

Drummers make sounds

by hitting their drums.

When we talk and sing, air passes through our vocal cords. The air makes them vibrate.

These kids sing in their school choir.

We use air to make vibrations in wind and brass instruments.

These students play their trumpets by blowing air into them.

Friction can also make things vibrate. Friction is caused when two things rub against each other.

You hear a sound when you rub your hands together.

When a bow rubs on a violin string, the violin makes a sound.

How many sounds

have you made today?

Activity
Seeing Sound

We use our ears to hear sounds. Inside an ear is a thin part called the eardrum. Sound waves make the eardrum vibrate. These vibrations are turned into messages for our brain.

Try this activity to see how our eardrum vibrates.

What you need:

a scissors

a balloon

a glass

a rubber band

a pinch of sugar

What you do:

1. Cut off the bottom of the balloon. This should make the balloon able to stretch over the top of the glass.

2. Stretch the top of the balloon tightly over the glass. Use the rubber band to hold the balloon tightly to the glass.

3. Set the glass on a firm surface. Put a little bit of sugar on top of the balloon.

4. Make loud noises like shouting or clapping near the cup. Watch how the sugar bounces as the sound waves make the balloon vibrate.

5. Experiment with different noises and with different distances from the cup. Do they make the sugar bounce more or less?

Glossary

friction: a force that slows things down or makes them stop. Rubbing creates friction.

gas: a substance that will spread to fill any space that contains it

liquid: a wet substance that you can pour

pitch: the highness or lowness of a sound

reflect: to bounce back

solid: a substance that has a definite shape

vibrate: to move back and forth quickly

vocal cords: parts of the throat that let a person talk or sing when air is breathed out, causing them to vibrate

Further Reading

BBC Schools Science Clips: Sound and Hearing
http://www.bbc.co.uk/schools/scienceclips/ages/5_6/
sound_hearing.shtml

Boothroyd, Jennifer. *What Is Hearing?*
Minneapolis: Lerner Publications Company, 2010.

Exploratorium: Listen Online Activities
http://exploratorium.com/listen/online_try.php

Mahaney, Ian F. *Sound Waves*. New York: Rosen,
2007.

The NASA Sci-Files: Sound Activities
http://scifiles.larc.nasa.gov/text/kids/D_Lab/acts_
sound.html

Walker, Sally M. *Sound*. Minneapolis:
Lerner Publications Company, 2006.

Index

Photo Acknowledgments

The images in this book are used with the permission of: © Juniors Bildarchiv/Alamy, p. 1; © iStockphoto.com/Nicole S. Young, p. 2; © Glow Images, inc./SuperStock, p. 4; © Elmari Joubert/Greatstock Photographic Library/Alamy, p. 5; © Mira/Alamy, p. 6; © Greg Ryan/Alamy, p. 7; © Image Source/Getty Images, p. 8; © Pixel Pusher Images/Alamy, p. 9; © Masa Ushioda/Alamy, p. 10; © Wim van den Heever/Tetra Images/Alamy, p. 11; © Ted Foxx/Alamy, p. 12; © C Squared Studios/Getty Images, p. 13; © Comstock Images/Getty Images, p. 14 (left); © Ron Levine/Digital Vision/Getty Images, p. 14 (right); © Ray Art Graphics/Alamy, p. 15; © Andersen Ross/Blend Images/Getty Images, p. 16; © Polka Dot Images/Photolibrary, p. 17; © SW Productions/Photodisc/Getty Images, p. 18; © Victoria Snowber/Digital Vision/Getty Images, p. 19; © zelijkosantrac/Shutterstock Images, p. 20; © Glow Images RM/Glow Images, p. 21; © Dennis MacDonald/Alamy, p. 22; © Symphonie Ltd/Cultura/Getty Images, p. 23; © Richard Baker/Alamy, p. 24; © Richard G. Bingham II/Alamy, p. 25; © Peter Dazeley/Photodisc/Getty Images, p. 26; © Big Cheese Photo/SuperStock, p. 27; © Alphababy/Dreamstime.com p. 28 (left); © iStockphoto.com/Iaroslav Danylchenko pp. 28 (right), © iStockphoto.com/Tobias Helbig p. 29 (middle); © iStockphoto.com/Scott Hogge p. 29 (left); © Les Cunliffe/Dreamstime.com p. 29 (right); © Gbh007/Dreamstime.com, p. 30; © Jaimee Itagaki/Red Images, LLC/Alamy, p. 31.

Front cover: © Image Source/Getty Images (girl listening to sea shell); © Design Pics/Ron Nickel/Getty Images (boy with cymbals); © iStockphoto.com/Fertnig (boy with guitar).